BOOK 3

Policy and Ethics Issues For Green Businesses

I0484197

Shel Horowitz

Green and Profitable Book 3: Policy and Ethics Issues for Green Business

ISBN-13: 978-1511419291
ISBN-10: 1511419296

Printed in the United States of America
10, 9, 8, 7, 6, 5, 4, 3, 2

Published by AWM Books - Hadley, MA

Contents

How Do You Balance Conflicting Environmental Priorities?

What do you do when there's no clear eco-friendly choice—when you have to balance competing claims of environmental benefit against competing harms?

In January [2011], I spoke at the Sustainable Foods Summit in San Francisco. My challenge to the other attenders was to achieve a food system that combines the artisan quality and chemical/petroleum independence of pre-20th century food production with the massive volume and ability to feed hungry people of the 20th century Green Revolution, while achieving the distribution necessary to end hunger.

Conflicting Priorities

That sounds great, in theory. But how do we get there? And what trade-offs do we have to make along the way?

Some of the other speakers had their own ideas about the rocky road ahead, not just in food sustainability but a host of related issues. Among the many concerns they raised:

✓ Is it better to switch to no–till farming, which dramatically alleviates soil erosion but is very difficult to do without herbicides—or to build up soil quality naturally through organic or biodynamic methods, and hope that the soil doesn't blow away in the meantime?

✓ What is the real benefit of using biodegradable plastics (such as compostable cutlery or packaging) if the sources of corn or potatoes for these plastics are genetically modified plants? And when food is scarce in many parts of the world, do we really want to divert cropland from food to plastic (or energy) production?

✓ Which is more sustainable: a lightweight plastic bag made from virgin materials (i.e., petroleum), or a plastic clamshell using 40 times as much material, but made from recycled water bottles?

Is there a "right answer" to these kinds of questions? The answer is situational. For the wheat growers of Washington State where a foot of topsoil has disappeared in the last 40 years, the no-till method sounds pretty compelling. In a different landscape, ravaged by chemical pollution, the organic argument would probably win out.

When the Benefits Line Up

Of course, there are many situations where a clearer path exists. If all the stars align in a single direction, the choice is easy. For instance, the conference heard from dairy cooperative Organic Valley's Theresa Marquez about the benefits of their approach: Organic farming creates richer and darker soil that is far better able to hold water and nutrients...organic cows fed a diet high in flaxseed oil produce more of the essential nutrient Omega-3 while decreasing the output of methane (a greenhouse gas linked even more heavily to global warming than carbon dioxide)—and they typically live up to three times longer than conventional-agriculture cows, which allows farms to be economically sustainable as well.

Marquez also noted that many of her member farms are planting some acreage in oilseed crops such as sunflowers, which can power a farm's trucks and tractors, feed its livestock and generate revenues.

The Challenges We Already Meet

Other speakers provided hope for meeting those difficult challenges mentioned earlier, by showing how their organizations are already surmounting equally difficult challenges. For example, Maisie Greenawalt of Bon Appetit Management Company (a food service provider to college, corporate, and organization cafeterias) inspired attenders with stories of converting institutional food service from slop to gourmet treats with fresh ingredients, and being profitable even while allowing college students unlimited trips to the (expensive, locally sourced, naturally raised non-antibiotic-treated beef) burger bar.

Not all sustainable food initiatives are local, of course. Fair trade—whose products often cross international borders—was also a much-discussed. From its beginnings in coffee, fair trade has olive oil, herbs, tea, cocoa, sugar, bananas, and many others. Fair trade ensures that the farmer makes a decent livelihood and has good working conditions, and the fair trade movement is spreading into such areas as bridge loans for farmers who only get paid once a year.

And more and more companies are producing goods that are not only fairly traded but also organic, providing sustainability not only to the farmers but to consumers as well.

Big…Or Little?

While once the province of tiny little artisan firms, these products and processes are breaking out of their niches. More and more of the major players in the food industry are making shelf space or production line space for organic, natural, and fairly traded goods, and many of the smaller companies have been bought up by industry giants. While this came up frequently at the conference, questions about the roles of multinationals versus tiny independents will have to wait for another time.

Fukushima Accidents Make It Clear: We Need Safe Energy Policies, World–Wide

Among many environmentalists and politicians, even some who ought to know better, it's been an axiom that we need nuclear power, because coal is so dirty and toxic and contributes so heavily to climate heating.

Unfortunately, nuclear is also dirty and toxic, as well as extremely dangerous. And despite its claims, it's far from carbon-neutral when you look at the whole fuel cycle. Those who looked closely, long before the tsunami wrecked the Fukushima Daiichi six-reactor complex, have been opposing nuclear power for decades.

Problems with Nuclear

Here are just a few of the many severe problems with reliance on nuclear:

✓ If a plant has a major problem, and has to be removed from service permanently, it causes disruption in the energy systems of the communities that depend on it, because a lot of power generation is taken off the grid at once—and sinks enormous amounts of unrecoverable capital.

In the case of Daiichi, most of those reactors can never be used again.

✓ The consequences of failure can be extremely severe (ask the people who used to live near Chernobyl, where a large swath of land remains uninhabitable after 25 years)—and the risk factors are numerous: not just earthquakes, tsunamis, hurricanes, and terrorism, but also component failure, and the lovely little thing called "human error" (both of which were factors in Fukushima, Chernobyl, and Three Mile Island).

✓ In many countries (including the United States, massive insurance subsidies and liability caps transfer almost all the risk from the utilities to ratepayers and area residents. If there's an accident don't expect to collect more than pennies on the dollar, if you get anything at all.

✓ Over the entire fuel cycle, starting with mining uranium and ending with attempting to find a solution for safe storage of nuclear waste, the process requires enormous energy inputs and excretes carbon, so the actual gains in usable power and greenhouse gas reduction are very tiny, if they exist at all. One study I've seen, by John J. Berger, states that from 1960–76, the nuclear power "generation" industry actually *consumed five times as much power as it generated*. I cited this study in my first book, Nuclear Lessons, published all the way back in 1980. For this, we're risking our future?

✓ And don't forget: there is no permanent solution to storage of radioactive waste, requiring isolation from the environment for up to a quarter of a million years. Considering that the oldest objects passed down to us are only about 40,000 years old, and that no human language has been around for even 5000 years, I have serious doubts about this.

Problems with Coal

OK, so what about coal?

✓ Just in the U.S., 104,722 coal mine workers were killed on the job in the past 110 years, an average of 952 deaths per year. In China, 2,433 miners were killed in 2010 alone.

✓ Much more sobering: in these two countries combined, a shocking 530,000 people reportedly die every year from coal-pollution-related diseases. Extrapolating worldwide, that means coal is responsible for millions of deaths per year. Clearly not sustainable.

The *Real* Alternatives

What, then, is the solution to our energy needs? It lies in the arms of good old Mother Nature.

Clean, renewable, non-destructive energy sources like solar, hydro, geothermal, wind, and even exotic sources like molecular or magnetic power can generate enough power so we can dispense with both coal and nuclear (as well as other polluting, greenhouse-gas-generating fuels like wood, which are renewable but not sustainable).

But in order to do so, we need to rethink the way we do energy. I propose three basic principles:

Energy should be generated close to or at the place where it will be used, to minimize friction and transmission losses.

Small-scale systems cause much fewer negative environmental consequences than large ones (for instance, in-river hydro that lets the water keep flowing is far more environmentally benign than large dams).

"Negawatts" and "negabarrels"—the energy we save by increasing our energy efficiency—can account for reductions of 50 percent or more in our energy needs.

So...how can we Green And Profitable entrepreneurs move this rethinking forward? For starters, we can make sure we've had recent energy audits at our businesses and homes, and have implemented many of the suggestions. We can look at  ways to conserve, and to use locally generated clean, renewable power. And we can create social pressure through our trade associations, our customer networks, and our purchasing to move away from every kind of unsustainable power source to the sustainable ones.

Sources:

Net loss of power from nuclear: Berger, John J. *Nuclear Power: The Univable Option* (New York: Dell, 1977, pp. 150-151, cited in Curtis, Richard, Elizabeth Hogan, Shel Horowitz. *Nuclear Lessons: An Examination of Nuclear Power's Safety, Economic, and Political Record* (Harrisburg: Stackpole, 1980, p. 90)

US coal mining fatalities: http://www.msha.gov/stats/centurystats/coalstats.asp

China coal mining fatalities: http://www.rfa.org/english/energy_watch/deaths-03072011114504.html

Coal pollution deaths in US and China: http://nextbigfuture.com/2008/03/deaths-per-twh-for-all-energy-sources.html

Energy savings from negawatts/negabarrels: http://wn.com/amory_lovins_we_must_win_the_oil_endgame

The terms "negawatts" and "negabarrels" were popularized by physicist Amory Lovins, founder of he green energy think-tank Rocky Mountain Institute.

How to Jumpstart the Renewable Economy Worldwide

You may have read about the Marshall Plan, which restarted the economy of Europe following World War II.

With the threat of catastrophic climate change hovering over our heads, and with the economy still in tatters in many parts of the world, I suggest a worldwide Marshall Plan-style initiative. Let's stave off global warming, create jobs, put significant discretionary spending money into  the hands of citizens, and lower energy prices—all at no net cost to the taxpayers, property owners, and renters.

Strategies would include lowering the price of clean technology by increasing demand...making energy-saving technology accessible to low- and middle-income people (including renters), and using the money saved to spur sustainable economic development. The plan, which I'd hope would be adopted by national, regional, and local governments around the world, would have these components:

1. Effective immediately, starting with any plans proposed and not yet approved, all government or government-funded construction would be required to generate at least as much energy as it consumes, through clean and renewable technologies, such as solar, wind, small-scale hydro, magnetic, tidal, bacterial, and deep conservation (this is not a comprehensive list).

If compromise is necessary, aim for 10 percent or less energy consumption compared with traditional nongreen buildings serving the same purpose.

Technologies must be both clean and renewable, which means they cannot be based in fossil fuels, nuclear, or most types of biomass.

2. As prices come down due to increased demand and economies of scale, locally administered government programs make renewable and clean technologies available to people who can't afford them, but in ways that are financially self-supporting.

For example, governments and utilities can join forces to set up lease-back programs. The company that installs an alternative energy system maintains ownership, but leases the energy back to the homeowner or tenant. Or the government guarantees loans that enable homeowners to purchase the systems and automatically pay back the loans out of the energy savings.

3. The new government buildings save government agencies enormous amounts of money in utilities. Those savings are earmarked to retrofit existing government buildings.

4. As the private sector repays the loans or buys the leased energy, that money becomes available to retrofit nongovernment buildings

Large-scale implementation would bring down the price...make it affordable to every homeowner...reduce or eliminate dependence on foreign oil and uranium...reduce CO_2 buildup and thus global warming. When, planet-wide, we see our rooftops as an energy (and possibly food) resource, and have programs in place to make these systems affordable to those without capital, we can eliminate oil dependence and reduce carbon emissions/global warming.

By outfitting every government building and providing means for low-income people to solarize, we can:

✓ Bring prices way down and make clean renewable energy more affordable to middle-income homeowners

✓ Free up capital currently spent on fossil fuels for economic development

✓ Create tens of thousands of new short-term jobs

✓ Reduce dependence on foreign oil

✓ Reduce pressure to "solve" our energy shortage through environmentally disastrous initiatives like tar-sands oil, fracking, and nuclear

✓ Slow or perhaps even reverse catastrophic climate change

We constantly hear dire predictions of what will happen if we don't address the carbon issue right away. Yet, even modest initiatives get caught in political wrangling and die a quick death. Because this program is essentially self-funding, and uses the workings of the free market to create affordable alternatives for the less wealthy, it should be politically easier to accomplish than other proposals—perhaps even in time to prevent climate catastrophe.

Meanwhile, the groundwork for this kind of international cooperation has already been laid. As one example, Put Solar On It <putsolaron.it>, an international initiative to get world leaders to solarize their presidential palaces, could be a natural organizing platform to expand from residences of heads of state to all government buildings. India, Chile, and the Maldives are among those who have already started solarizing their presidential palaces, and the U.S. could easily replace the solar panels that were installed on the White House all the way back in 1979 (unfortunately removed by the subsequent president). Expanding to the hundreds of thousands of other government buildings is a logical next step.

Let's show some initiative and gumption, put aside our cultural differences, and get this done.

Greenwashing, Nuclear Power, and You

When I'm interviewed on radio, I'm almost invariably asked about greenwashing, and about being able to tell the difference between real green actions and fake ones.

Usually, I respond by citing the nuclear power industry as an example of how not to do green messaging.

Nuclear power's proponents claim it's a green technology, because spinning the turbines creates less carbon dioxide than spinning turbines using oil, coal, or natural gas. But that argument doesn't hold up  to scrutiny; when you look at the entire cycle, from mining and milling the uranium through assembling it into nuclear fuel, transporting it across vast distances, loading it into the power plant, actually operating the plant, and then removing it afterwards, you find a significant carbon footprint (not to mention considerable consumption of energy).

And we don't even know the carbon impact of storing the waste long-term in complete isolation from the environment (we're talking about a quarter of a million years)—because the technology to do that doesn't even exist.

And then we've got the little matter of radiation. Dozens of isotopes are produced in the nuclear cycle, some of them not found in nature, and most of them highly toxic and carcinogenic.

This is all part of routine operation. When things go wrong, the negative environmental impact goes up by orders of magnitude. More than a quarter-century after the Chernobyl accident, vast areas of the Ukraine are still uninhabitable (including some parts that had been among the best farmland in Eastern Europe). And it's still not clear if a comparable disaster will occur at Fukushima-Dai'ichi, where the fuel rods from the #4 reactor are still in grave danger of catastrophic failure, and where at least two reactors melted down during the accident.

And if you think nuclear accidents only happen once in a long while, consider this: We've heard about Three Mile Island, Chernobyl, and now, the second (2011) major failures at Fukushima. But those are only the most publicized in a long line of accidents at nuclear power plants and related facilities. From 1952 to 2009, there were at least 99 accidents causing loss of life or at least USD $50,000 in property damage, and that does not count the Fukushima accidents in 2010 and 2011.

Chernobyl alone, according to European reports, has caused a shocking 1 million deaths and $500,000,000,000 in property damage—and that's before long-latency cancers start to show up.

I wouldn't call that green!

So what does this mean for those of us in the green marketing world?

First, we have an obligation to protect our industry by confronting this falsehood. As some countries are drawing away from nuclear power, others (including the US) still embrace it. We need to use the full weight of our marketing skills to get the message out that nuclear is the most ungreen technology ever created, that it is not a solution. And that we have plenty of solutions that are appropriate, using renewable, nonpolluting, safe technologies such as human-scale solar, wind, hydro, tidal, and geothermal.

Second and even more importantly, we have an obligation to our planet to protect ourselves from this menace. Whenever new nuclear power (or renewal of existing nuclear power) is proposed, we need to be there opposing it, demonstrating not only the greenwashing lies but the cost to our health, safety, and even our freedom.

If you'd like to know more, I'll send you the ten-page update I wrote when my 1980 book was reprinted in Japan, post-Fukushima (which includes reference citations). Please write to me, shel AT greenandprofitable.com, with the subject line "Send 2011 Nuke Intro."

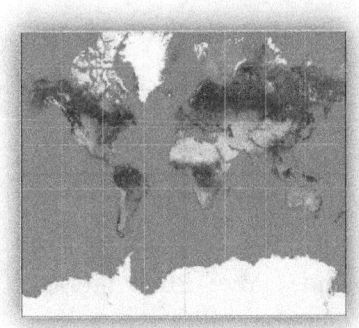

Shifting to a Global Perspective

As a child growing up in the United States of the 1960s and 1970s, I knew only one map of the world: the Mercator projection that makes the polar regions look bigger, and the equatorial areas smaller, than their actual relative sizes. Usually, the Americas were in the center with eastern Asia and Australia on the left—and Europe, Africa, and western Asia on the right; once in a while, I'd see a version that put Europe and Africa in the center, Asia connected to it on the right, and Greenland and the Americas across the Atlantic to the left—the version that most European students my age and older grew up with.

In these maps, Greenland appears to be bigger than Australia and India combined; Greenland actually appears to be larger than Africa. In reality, Africa, at 30,065,000 sq km (11,608,161.4 square miles), is 14 times the size of Greenland.

It's impossible to accurately project a round sphere like the earth onto a rectangle. Something has to give. In Mercator projections, the shapes of land masses are pretty accurate—but the sizes are wildly distorted.

But in the Peters projection developed much later (in 1974), those distortions are reversed. Land masses show their relative size, but the shapes are barely recognizable. The first time I saw a Peters map,

probably about 30 years ago, it was a shock. It changed the way I think about the world.

And I love Buckminster Fuller's Dymaxion Map, centered on the North Pole, which keeps both sizes and shapes of landmasses accurate, but does very strange things to the distances between continents. In Fuller's map, the world's land masses appear as a nearly-connected chain, surrounded by a single ocean. Australia, Eurasia, and Africa show deep commonalities of interest, while North America appears as close to Europe as to South America.

Dymaxion, Peters and Mercator are only three of a wide range of global maps. You can make a map that has the top in any direction; here, for instance, are several with south at the top, giving prominence to South America, southern Africa, and Australia: flourish.org/upsidedownmap

And since the Earth is a sphere, you can also make a map with the center at any point you like; I've seen various maps with Toronto, Tokyo, and Mecca at the center.

So, you ask—what on Earth does this have to do with profitable green business? Quite a bit, actually.

✓ How we map the world influences our worldview.

For European and North American explorers and conquerors, growing up with a view of Africa as smaller than Greenland perhaps made it easier to minimize the many accomplishments of African cultures, dehumanize the dark-skinned people of Africa as inferior—and then intellectually justify the history of imperialism and exploitation that followed.

In today's multicultural world, understanding the importance of the Global South helps us remember that, for example, we can't just ship off our toxic byproducts and bury them in some developing country.

- ✓ The creativity of these different maps and the thousands of other variations reminds us that sometimes, simple answers to complex problems such as environmental devastation are a lot easier to see if we shift our perspective (as we talked about in last month's column on simple elegance).

- ✓ Maps can show much more than position.

"Heat map"-style infographics can show relative accomplishments, population, natural resources and other factors—and green entrepreneurs can use these as planning tools that take environmental and social factors into consideration

In short, maps, as windows on the natural and the human-created worlds, serve different purposes. Mercator was a very appropriate choice for 17th- and 18th-century sailors wanting the easiest transit between Europe and North America, while Dymaxion is perfect to bring home Fuller's concept of "Spaceship Earth"—an interconnected single ecosystem.

For a detailed and fascinating look at how maps shape our thinking, I strongly recommend **Seeing Through Maps: Many Ways to See the World**, by Denis Wood, Ward L. Kaiser, and Bob Abramms, ODTMaps.com/detail.asp_Q_product_id_E_STM-2-BKttty

How to Influence Public Officials on Environmental Issues

As both a marketing consultant and environmental activist, I'm accustomed to writing or presenting words that convince the public to change their positions—or their brands—and to take action based on my writing or speaking.

To do this, I will use my powers of persuasion and a wide range of language aimed at moving different types of people forward toward a common agenda. My arguments will typically be a mix of emotion and intellect, of appeals to self-interest and appeals to the common good.

But I've learned over the years that when the goal is influencing public officials, the rules and strategies are different.

For one thing, when government officials take testimony on an issue, they typically have a very narrow scope. In fact, they're often not even allowed to consider anything outside their purview (this is one of the reasons why change involving action by government enforcement agencies or getting new laws passed can be frustratingly slow). So big, sweeping appeals along broad issues have little effect.

Last month, I wanted to weigh in before a government body on one of those big-picture issues. I submitted testimony to a state government agency on whether it should issue a certain permit to a nuclear power plant. I wanted to address the much wider issue of nuclear power plant safety—but I had to do it within the narrow confines of what the board could address.

I think my testimony makes an instructive example of how to influence governments—so let me point out a few things about my testimony
(which I've posted at shelhorowitz.com/go/nucleartestimony):

- ✓ Establish credentials—why it's your right to give testimony.

Right at the beginning, I note that I've written three relevant books—and this is especially important since I'm not a resident of the state where the plant is located. Credentials don't have to be formal, though. Yours might be "resident within the evacuation zone" or "parent of a special-needs child."

- ✓ Focus on the issue the agency can act on.

The hearing was about whether the state should grant the nuke a new Certificate of Public Good. So very early, I looked at what it means to provide public good—and then I referred back to this concept several times, including the last sentence.

- ✓ Use an objective–sounding, intelligent tone.

Not the time for screaming hype or unsubstantiated accusations.

✓ Respect their knowledge and intelligence.

Notice that I didn't explain the Price-Anderson Act; I simply referenced it with an "as you know."

✓ Provide a framework for addressing the wider
  issues.

By US federal law, the federal Nuclear Regulatory Commission has jurisdiction over the safety of nuclear power plants. But the state of Vermont can take economic factors into account when evaluating whether the plant serves a public good—so I anchored all my safety arguments in their impact on the state's economy and overtly stated that this is why I was bringing up the safety issues.

✓ Back up your claims and cite sources.

I cite three books, the plant's own accident report, one third-party scientific report, and two top-tier newspaper articles (from the New York Times and Washington Post).

✓ Clearly state the desired action the agency should
  take, ideally quite early in your remarks.

In this case, I want the Public Service Board to deny the Certificate of Pubic Good requested by Entergy, and I say so very specifically in the second sentence: "Like the majority of people who have come before you to testify, I ask that you deny the Certificate of Public Good for Entergy for the continued operation of the Vermont Yankee nuclear power plant."

- ✓ Use "social proof"—demonstrate that lots of people agree with you.

Look again at the quote from my testimony in the previous paragraph: the first half of the sentence is all about social proof; the second half tells them what I want them to do.

- ✓ Be organized ahead of time, and be conscious of time limits if speaking in person, and be willing to provide your full, extended testimony in writing.

I had an outline with me of points I could make within two minutes. It would not have been nearly as complete, but it would have hit the important points.

For maximum impact, make copies of your statement available to the media and to the public. My statement is published on my website, and thus my potential audience is a lot bigger than the three members of the Public Service Board.

Green Advocates Must Convince the Other Side
with Economic Arguments

Last month, one town away from me, there was a big dustup when the city decided to spray some athletic fields with Roundup. In addition to concerns about the health effects on the children who'd be playing on those fields, the parcel happens to directly about a commercial organic farm—one about to receive USDA organic certification, which means that it's been chemical-free for three years.

I sent a letter to the Mayor, selected members of the City Council, the Recreation Department, and the Chair of the Board of Public Works. I also copied a reporter at the local paper.

I'm going to share the relevant portions of that e-mail with you, then discuss why I framed it as I did—because there are many lessons in advocacy here, not only in the public sphere, but in dealing with any stakeholders on sustainability issues:

As a customer of Crimson & Clover Farm and many other organic farms in the area...a 26-1/2-year property owner in Northampton (through this past April), and an internationally recognized expert in the marketing of green products and services, I urge you in the strongest possible terms to BLOCK the proposed spraying of Roundup.

You are no doubt aware of the growing importance of agritourism and ecotourism in Northampton and the Pioneer Valley—which includes at least two lodging establishments within the City that specifically cater to a green clientele (Starlight Lama and Trailside B&Bs). Much in that sector has to do with a creating and sustaining a culture of support for local organic foods that includes both farmers and consumers. I even use the Valley as an example in my speaking and writing on green business, nationally and internationally.

—> Spraying Roundup—a pesticide whose long-term safety is highly questionable—could have severe deleterious effects on Crimson & Clover and Grow Food Northampton.

Spraying could easily drift onto the wrong fields and/or contaminate nearby water, resulting in a loss of Crimson & Clover's organic certification, a loss of customers—I am one who would not knowingly buy from a farm tainted by Roundup—and *possible lawsuits* for interfering with the livelihood of another.

And did you know that in addition to selling Roundup, Monsanto sells Roundup-tolerant GMO seeds, and then sues farmers whose fields get contaminated with them for using the seeds without permission? I have a lot of trouble with their ethics. Roundup furthers Monsanto's actions to crush local and organic agriculture...

Meanwhile, I hope you will use your influence to prevent this potential can of worms from ever being opened—and I hope to greet the three of you at the rally at Crimson & Clover tomorrow afternoon.

Why This Approach?

Paragraph 1: Establishing my credentials.

I am affected by what affects this farm, because I am a customer. I owned a home in that town for a long period of time. And I happen to have validated expertise in the subject. But if you don't have textbook credentials, you can work with what you have. For instance, you could speak as a property owner, parent, and purchaser of organic foods.

Paragraph 2: Identifying organic agriculture as an important and growing sector in the local economy.

This is critical; organic agriculture is too often seen as marginal and trivial. I shown that tax-paying businesses are affected by the city's decision—and that the region has been a model for the rest of the country and even the world.

Paragraphs 3 and 4: Demonstrating the potential negative economic consequences to the affected business, *and* to the city.

All municipalities in my area are strapped for cash. This city even went through a very contentious vote to raise taxes just a few months ago, to avoid severe layoffs across many departments.

Avoiding adding to that burden with preventable lawsuits is an argument to make the government pay attention.

Paragraph 5: The wider context.

In my writing and speaking, I often talk about combining self-interest and planetary interest messages. This is the planetary part. Monsanto's frequent legal challenges to farmers whose fields were contaminated by drift is a serious problem in the organic farming world.

Paragraph 6: Offering a positive step.

I conclude the letter with something these officials can do to show their solidarity and gain public support.

Results: One City Councilor did attend the rally. And the Mayor announced a compromise plan that put a no-spray buffer around the edge. Without the buffer on city land, the organic farm would have had to sacrifice three acres for its own buffer in order to obtain that organic certification. While it wasn't the ideal outcome, it was much better than the original plan, and shows the power of organizing along economic interest.

Polarization vs. Unification

Is polarization an effective strategy for change?

I've felt for decades that confronting the power structure—and shaking up the "truths" that people might hold dear—is essential to creating the better world we all seek.

But by itself, that isn't enough. Yes, if you want to accomplish deep change, you need polarizers to create awareness and shake up the status quo—and you also need unifiers to put the shattered pieces back together and facilitate forward movement. Without both halves, the yin and the yang of organizing, very little actually changes, either in the business world or in the streets.

I've played both roles at various times. For about the last 20 years, I've been much more about creating unity and moving the larger world to social change—in many cases, using business to enable that change.

Years earlier, I'd been a polarizer. I remember a conversation in early 1976, when I was 19. I don't remember what I'd said, but my listener, probably 20 years older than me, turned to me and asked, "Why are you so bitter?"

I'd never thought of myself as bitter. Angry, certainly. The Vietnam war had been raging until the previous year. My government had been killing or jailing many agents of social change. The business community seemed a heartless, soulless place that cared only for profits—I've obviously learned a different truth since then—and the environment was visibly in jeopardy. The more we worked for a better world, the farther away it seemed.

Yet, even then, I had at least a bit of hope—but apparently, I wasn't very good at conveying that hope. I have a whole lot more hope now than I did 38 years ago. Maybe that's why lately I've been much more drawn to building consensuses than to shattering doctrines.

I believe that we make change by harnessing those opposites into something greater than either part. Perhaps you need the doom-and-gloom alarmism of people like anti-nuclear activist Dr. Helen Caldicott of Australia or suburbia-is-dying prophet James Kunstler of

the United States before people will respond to the optimism of people like energy futurist Amory Lovins and the late bacterial scholar Lynn Margulis. Perhaps you need the loud unkempt rebels of the Occupy movement to hear the quiet voices of Israeli and Palestinian families joining hands in mutual condolence  and holding a banner together for peace.

Yes, we need to know the terrible consequences of nonaction, of allowing a planet in crisis to deepen that crisis. But if we're going to move out of that crisis, that needs a platform too. Before people reach the depth of despair, extend the hand up they need to get back into turning the existing into the possible, and the possible into the amazing.

In every aspect of modern life—energy, agriculture, transportation, construction, waste reduction, to name just a few—brilliant minds are at work solving all those huge problems. We know so much more about all of this than we used to know.

Those advances are everywhere you look in the green world. Think about the order-of-magnitude increase in the efficiency of comparably priced photovoltaic panels just in the past ten years. Think about organic agriculture—

not only vastly more productive, but producing food that looks better and tastes better, and using new models of distribution such as Community Supported Agriculture. Think about Zero waste, making gains in using every resource more efficiently. And most of all, think of how the environmental movement has shifted the consciousness of ordinary people around the world—think of the impact that you've had, in your own work.

Could those gains have been accomplished while swimming in a cold sea of negativity, fatalism, and beating ourselves up for killing the world? No; in a climate that drives away optimism and hope, depression leads to paralysis. But could those gains have been accomplished in a Polyanna climate of nothing's ever wrong? No, again; there would be no incentive to improve.

Let's end this business column with a business example. 30 years ago, I got my first computer, an original 128K Apple Macintosh. A major advance in both computing power and usability, this state-of-the-art machine had just 128 kilobytes—not megabytes and certainly not gigabytes—of memory (twice what the IBM PC had at the time). It had no hard drive, just a single 400K disk drive. The tiny 9-inch (22.86 cm) display was black-and-white. To get online, I dialed up over a 300 bps modem and watched my text-only characters pour

slowly across the screen and into cyberspace. That machine, less powerful than any smart phone today, cost $3000 US.

Today, Apple is mainstream. But it's worth remembering that the Macintosh was quite deliberately polarizing. In the very first ad, a runner smashed a dictator's video monitor with a hammer. The later Mac vs. PC series continued the theme. Yet, the original Macintosh motto was the uniting "computer for the rest of us," and the company's greatest successes were built on very inclusive, ground-breaking, problem-solving products aimed squarely at the mainstream: the iPod, iPhone, and iPad.

Which role does your business play right now?

Sustainability is Not Enough

In the green world, we hear the terms sustainable or sustainability quite often. Sustainability is a good first step. But is that really all we want?

Not even close. Sustainability means making sure the status quo—the existing situation—can self-replicate. But keeping the current situation from getting worse doesn't mean it's getting better.

Experts put the safe level of carbon in the atmosphere at 350 parts per million. But the August 2014 figure was 397.01 parts per million, or 113 percent of what it should be. And it's probably not a coincidence that extreme weather events (floods, droughts, intense hurricanes, tsunamis, tornados, and such) have become both a lot more common and much more catastrophic.

The 14 years of the 21st century have included nine of the ten warmest years in the past 134 years; the sole 20th-century year in the hottest ten was 1998—almost into the 21st.

Our non-renewable resources are being depleted. Whether it's oil (used not only for energy but for most plastics), iron ore, bauxite (raw material for aluminum), or the rare-earth metals used to make products like cell phones, the raw materials that were highest quality and easiest to extract have already been harvested. The remaining materials are harder to extract, require more energy to process, and/or generate more pollution. Energy extraction methods like tar sands oil or fracking can wreak environmental devastation. Tar sands oil is dirty and low quality, scars the landscape, and requires enormous energy input. Fracking is more efficient and actually cheaper than the old methods, but puts our water supplies—our most precious resource—at risk. "Mountaintop removal" destroys whole ecosystems to get coal out of the ground.

Products and their components—even food—travel thousands of unnecessary miles. The deck seems stacked against truly local economies.

Our world takes enormous unnecessary risks by disregarding the Precautionary Principle and unleashing technologies whose effects are not known—like GMO foods—or that are known to be  potentially catastrophic—like nuclear power—because we use narrow cost-benefit analyses that only selectively count costs and disregard the complexities of lifecycles and disposal.

We want a world that's getting better. We want a world that's undoing the damage humans have caused to the planet. And I think it's safe to say that as green business owners, we want to be part of that healing.

So let's reframe the conversation. Let's stop talking about sustainability—and start talking in terms like "regeneration" and "restoration."

And let's create structures that empower businesses to combine the vision of what needs to change with the commitment to change it. Alternative business structures, from B-corporations to coops, are a first step. But beyond that, let's harness the profit motive to *get it done*.

In 2014, we should no longer put up with a world full of misery. Isn't it time to reward businesses that are working meaningfully to end hunger, poverty, war, and climate catastrophe while penalizing those that are stuck in the rapacious practices of the past?

I've expanded on some of these ideas in a 15-minute TED talk, "Impossible is a Dare: Business For a Better World." Please watch it (and see the slides) at; www.business-for-a-better-world.com/tedtalks

And please visit http://business-for-a-better-world.com, where you'll find the beginnings of resources to address and *solve* these issues, including the chance to nominate your favorite socially conscious business project so others can work on it too.

Source for August 2014 carbon level and hottest years: http://co2now.org/

* * *

I enjoyed writing this column from 2010 to 2014, and I think I provided very high value for those who read it. Unfortunately, I never got enough markets to make the project economically viable.

As I move in the direction of helping companies see the value in solving problems like hunger, poverty, war, and climate catastrophe, I can no longer afford the luxury of doing this column for the few markets that subscribed. So this will be the last issue for a while.

I'd love to bring it back, if I can get to a minimum number of subscribers each paying just $10 per month. If you have possible markets for me, please drop me a line at shel AT greenandprofitable.com with the subject "Column Market."

Disclaimer: The very observant among you may notice that some examples come up more than once. Keep in mind that this ebook is a compilation of a monthly column that ran for four years. I have organized the columns by topic rather than chronologically here, and as a result, columns that may have been years apart end up close to each other in the same ebook. Yes, some examples are repeated, but they were inserted to make different points, at different times. Please also note that nothing in this ebook series should be taken as legal or professional advice, and as in any situation, your results may vary as you implement the tips and ideas.

About Shel Horowitz and Business For a Better World

Green business profitability expert Shel Horowitz shows businesses how to profit both by going green and by addressing problems like hunger and poverty, war, violence, and catastrophic climate change. Active in both marketing and the environment since his teen years in the early 1970s, Shel is the award-winning author of eight books including long-running Amazon category bestseller *Guerrilla Marketing Goes Green*.

✓ As a consultant, Shel brings laser focus to turning problems into opportunities, opening new markets, and helping you identify potential partners.

✓ As a marketing and informational copywriter trained in journalism, Shel is known for his clear writing, ability to make technical concepts accessible, and his skill in telling "the story behind the story" to move people to action.

✓ As an international speaker and trainer, Shel combines dynamic vocal style with powerful graphics and gets his audiences actively involved. He's spoken at major business and environmental conferences in locations as diverse as Istanbul, Davos (Switzerland), and Honolulu.

After over a decade actively assisting green businesses with their marketing, Shel branched out in 2014 to help businesses seize profit opportunities in turning hunger and poverty into sufficiency, war and violence into peace, and catastrophic climate change into planetary balance—and helping individuals reclaim their power to actively create this better world.

Shel is happy to talk to you about helping in any of these areas. Reach him at 413-586-2388 (8 a.m. to 10 p.m. US Eastern Time), email shel AT greenandprofitable.com, or find him on Twitter @ShelHorowitz.

Shel also has a gift for you: a free copy of his ebook, *Painless Green: 111 Tips to Help the Environment, Lower Your Carbon Footprint, Cut Your Budget, and Improve Your Quality of Life—With No Negative Impact on Your Lifestyle*. To claim your free copy of this $9.95 ebook, visit PainlessGreenBook.com/earthday and use the code, G&Pebook.

One more set of gifts, FREE with your no-cost subscription to Shel Horowitz's monthly Clean and Green Newsletter:

- ✓ Seven Tips to Gain Marketing Traction as a Green Guerrilla

- ✓ Seven Weeks to a Greener Business: once a week for seven weeks, tips on going greener with printing, energy saving, waste reduction, water conservation, transportation, going deep–green, and of course, green marketing.

- ✓ Plus the informative monthly newsletter, published since 1997 and featuring a business tip or profile plus a book review each issue.

Sign up in the upper-right-hand corner at http://greenandprofitable.com.

www.ingramcontent.com/pod-product-compliance
Lightning Source LLC
Chambersburg PA
CBHW071013180526
45168CB00003B/1406